D0044472

A Circle in the Sky

Written by Zachary Wilson
Illustrated by JoAnn Adinolfi

Children's Press®
A Division of Scholastic Inc.
New York • Toronto • London • Auckland • Sydney
Mexico City • New Delhi • Hong Kong
Danbury, Connecticut

For my niece Elle.
—Z. W.

To Gemma, my little explorer.
—J. A.

Reading Consultant

Cecilia Minden-Cupp, PhD
Former Director of the Language and Literacy Program
Harvard Graduate School of Education
Cambridge, Massachusetts

Cover design: The Design Lab
Interior design: Herman Adler

Library of Congress Cataloging-in-Publication Data

Wilson, Zachary, 1975–
  A circle in the sky / by Zachary Wilson ; illustrated by JoAnn Adinolfi.
      p. cm. —(A rookie reader)
  Summary: A child puts together various simple shapes to build a rocket
that will fly to the moon.
    ISBN-10: 0-531-12570-X (lib. bdg.)   0-531-12589-0 (pbk.)
    ISBN-13: 978-0-531-12570-0 (lib. bdg.)   978-0-531-12589-2 (pbk.)
  [1. Shape—Fiction. 2. Rockets (Aeronautics)—Fiction. 3. Stories in
rhyme.] I. Adinolfi, JoAnn, ill. II. Title. III. Series.
   PZ8.3.W6998Cir 2006
   [E]—dc22   2006006755

2 3 4 5 6 7 8 9 10 R 16 15 14 13 12 11 10 09 08

I see a circle in the sky,
white and shining bright.

I have some shapes and want to build . .

4

a rocket to fly to
the moon tonight.

6

I will use a rectangle door . . .

so I can go inside.

I will use a circle window . . .

so I can see outside.

I will use a triangle top . . .

to point me to the sky.

18

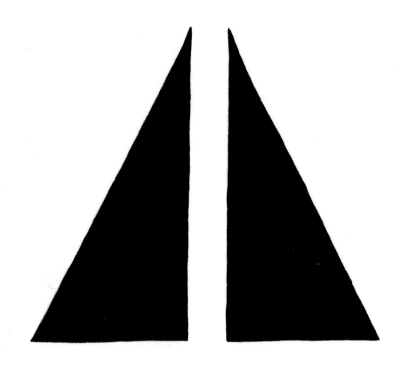

I will use triangle wings . . .

so my rocket ship can fly.

On the bottom I will use a square . . .

to push my rocket into the

27

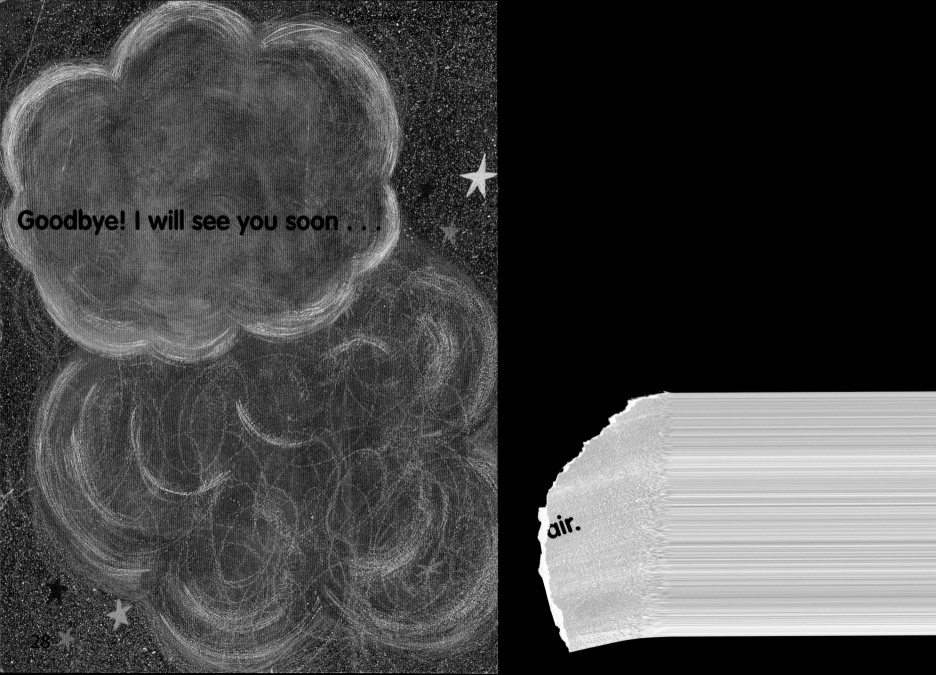

Goodbye! I will see you soon . . .

air.

when I get back from my trip to the moon

Word List (52 words)
(Words in **bold** are shapes.)

a	from	my	ship	**triangle**
air	get	on	sky	trip
and	go	outside	so	use
back	goodbye	point	some	want
bottom	have	push	soon	when
bright	I	**rectangle**	**square**	white
build	in	rocket	the	will
can	inside	see	to	window
circle	into	shapes	tonight	wings
floor	me	shining	top	you
fly	moon			

About the Author

Zach Wilson is an art teacher in New Jersey. He enjoys working with children of all ages and looks forward to writing more books.

About the Illustrator

JoAnn has illustrated many books for children. She was born and raised in Staten Island, New York, and now lives in Portsmouth, New Hampshire, with her husband and two children.

DA ODC 2010